The Concise Illustrated Book of
Steam Trains

Edited by D. Avery

GALLERY BOOKS
An imprint of W. H. Smith Publishers Inc.
112 Madison Avenue
New York, New York 10016

First published in the United States of
America by GALLERY BOOKS
An imprint of W. H. Smith Publishers Inc.
112 Madison Avenue
New York, New York 10016

ISBN 0-8317-7994-2

Printed in the German Democratic
Republic

*The Scarborough Spa Express headed by
the restored King Arthur Class No. 777 Sir
Lamiel.*

CONTENTS

CLASS A1 4-6-2

Country of Origin: Great Britain
Railway: London & North Eastern Railway (LNER)
Date: 1922
Length Overall: 21.46m (70ft 5in)
Total Weight: 150,909kg (332,000lb)
Cylinders: 3 508x660mm (20x26in)
Driving Wheels: 2.032m (6ft 8in)
Axle Load: 20,454kg (45,000lb)
Fuel: 8,181kg (18,000lb)
Grate Area: 3.8msq (41.25sq ft)
Water: 22,700lit (5,000gal) (6,000 US gal)
Heating Surface: 272msq (2,930sq ft)
Superheater: 49msq (525sq ft)
Steam Pressure: 12.6kg/cmsq (180psi)
Adhesive Weight: 61,136kg (134,500lb)
Tractive Effort: 13,333kg (29,385lb)

No. 4472, Flying Scotsman, *which is preserved at Steamtown Museum, Carnforth.*

The first Pacific locomotives to enter service in Great Britain were Gresley's Class A1 which remained in prestige passenger service until December 1965 when the last engine, British Railways No. 60041 *Salmon Trout,* was withdrawn.

Country of Origin: Great Britain
Railway: Great Western Railway (GWR)
Date: 1923
Length Overall: 19.863m (65ft 2in)
Total Weight: 128,863kg (283,500lb)
Cylinders: 4 406x660mm (16x26in)
Driving Wheels: 2.045m (6ft 8.5in)
Axle Load: 20,227kg (44,500lb)
Fuel: 6,136kg (13,500lb)
Grate Area: 2.81msq (30.3sq ft)
Water: 18,160lit (4,000gal) (4,800 US gal)
Heating Surface: 190msq (2,049sq ft)
Superheater: 24.4msq (263sq ft)
Steam Pressure: 15.8kg/cmsq (225psi)
Adhesive Weight: 60,681kg (133,500lb)
Tractive Effort: 14,182kg (31,625lb)

No. 4079, Pendennis Castle, *leaving Thackley Tunnel, Yorkshire, in September 1974.*

Churchward's successor as Chief Mechanical Engineer at the Great Western Railway, Charles Collett, originated the Castle Class. Designed around the Star Class locomotive, the Castles had much larger boilers. The first of these, *Caerphilly Castle*, No. 4073, entered service in August 1923 and is now an exhibit at the Science Museum, London. Subsequently 15 Star Class locomotives were converted to Castles, and over a period of 27 years no fewer than 170 Castle Class 4-6-0 locomotives entered service with Great Western. It was at one time the most powerful British locomotive, and gained the world speed record for steam locomotives when it achieved 131.5km/h (81.7mph) in 1932. The last Castle locomotive was withdrawn from service in July 1967. Seven engines have been preserved, of which three are in working order.

K-36 CLASS 2-8-2

Country of Origin: USA
Railway: Denver & Rio Grande Western Railroad (D&RGW)
Date: 1925
Length Overall: 20.802m (68ft 3in)
Total Weight: 130,227kg (286,500lb)
Cylinders: 2 508x609mm (20x24in)
Driving Wheels: 1.117m (3ft 8in)
Axle Load: 17,980kg (39,558lb)
Fuel: 7,272kg (16,000lb)
Grate Area: 3.7msq (40sq ft)
Water: 18,931lit (4,166gal) (5,000 US gal)
Heating Surface: 196msq (2,107sq ft)
Superheater: 53msq (575sq ft)
Steam Pressure: 13.7kg/cmsq (195psi)
Adhesive Weight: 65,386kg (143,850lb)
Tractive Effort: 16,425kg (36,200lb)

No. 2825 K-36 locomotive, built by the American Locomotive Company in 1923.

The K-36 2-8-2 Class locomotives, along with their sister narrow-gauge (914mm: 3ft) K-37 2-8-2s, were all built by the American Locomotive Company with the exception of ten K-36 locomotives which were supplied by Baldwin. The Denver and Rio Grande Western Railway Company went bankrupt during the Depression, and on coming out of receivership in 1947 it merged with the Denver and Saltlake Railroad to begin operating the famous California Zephyr service from Chicago to San Francisco in conjunction with the Western Pacific Railroad. They abandoned most of their narrow-gauge passenger lines, together with their K-36 locomotives and all other narrow-gauge rolling stock plus 103km (64 miles) of track, selling it off in 1968 to the State of Colorado and New Mexico who now run both K-36s and K-37s as a tourist railroad. This has now been renamed the Cumbres and Toltec Scenic Railroad.

Country of Origin: Great Britain
Railway: Southern Railway (SR)
Date: 1925
Length Overall: 20.244m (66ft 5in)
Total Weight: 141,136kg (310,500lb)
Cylinders: 2 521x711mm (20.5 x 28in)
Driving Wheels: 2.007m (6ft 7in)
Axle Load: 20,454kg (45,000lb)
Fuel: 5,000kg (11,000lb)
Grate Area: 2.8msq (30sq ft)
Water: 22,700lit (5,000gal) (6,000 US gal)
Heating Surface: 174.5msq (1,878sq ft)
Superheater: 31.3msq (337sq ft)
Steam Pressure: 14.1kg/cmsq (200psi)
Adhesive Weight: 61,136kg (134,500lb)
Tractive Effort: 11,485kg (25,320lb)

The King Arthur Class locomotive Sir Lamiel *climbs Church Fenton bank, Yorkshire.*

LSWR works at Eastleigh built 44 locomotives and the North British Locomotive Company of Glasgow built 30 King Arthur Class 4-6-0s which were employed by Southern Railway on their principal routes until replaced by the Lord Nelson Class.

Designed by Richard Maunsell, Chief Mechanical Engineer of Southern Railway, they were an improvement on the N15 Class 4-6-0s with improved combustion which was a consequence of the engine having both larger ashpans and large superheaters.

CLASS 01 4-6-2

Country of Origin: Germany
Railway: German State Railway (DR)
Date: 1926
Length Overall: 23.94m (78ft 6in)
Total Weight: 109,090kg (240,000lb)
excluding tender
Cylinders: 2 600x660mm (23.6x26.0in)
Driving Wheels: 2m (6ft 6.7in)
Axle Load: 20,227kg (44,500lb)
Fuel: 10,000kg (22,000lb)
Grate Area: 4.41msq (47.5sq ft)
Water: 34,050lit (7,500gal) (9,000 US gal)
Heating Surface: 247.3msq (2,661sq ft)
Superheater: 85msq (915sq ft)
Steam Pressure: 16kg/cmsq (228psi)
Adhesive Weight: 59,318kg (130,500lb)
Tractive Effort: 16,160kg (35,610lb)

A West German Pacific Class 01 crosses the River Moselle.

AEG and Börsig of Berlin built 231 Class 01 4-6-2 locomotives between them prior to the Second World War. The engines, fitted with bar frames and round-topped copper fireboxes, were produced for the German State Railway, which had been established in 1922. Dr R. P. Wagner, who was in charge of the Central Locomotive Design Section, tested two different Pacific Class locomotives: the 2-cylinder Class 01 and a 4-cylinder compound Class 02. The Class 01 was the victor because its running costs were lower and it was an easier locomotive to maintain. The Class 01 locomotives remained in service after the Second World War when 171 locomotives were handed over to West Germany and a further 70 to East Germany. They remained in service in West Germany until 1973.

Country of Origin: USA
Railway: Union Pacific Railroad (UP)
Date: 1926
Length Overall: 31.267m (102ft 7in)
Total Weight: 35,545kg (782,000lb)
Cylinders: 2 685x812mm (27x32in);
1 685x787mm (27x31in)
Driving Wheels: 1.70m (5ft 7in)
Axle Load: 27,272kg (60,000lb)
Fuel: 19,090kg (42,000lb)
Grate Area: 10msq (108sq ft)
Water: 56,750lit (12,500gal) (15,000 US gal)
Heating Surface: 544msq (5,853sq ft)
Superheater: 238msq (2,560sq ft)
Steam Pressure: 15.5kg/cmsq (220psi)
Adhesive Weight: 16,136kg (355,000lb)
Tractive Effort: 43,852kg (96,650lb)

No. 9032 at Topeka, Kansas in 1952.

An enormous 12-coupled locomotive, of which 88 were built for Union Pacific, this was the largest non-articulated locomotive ever constructed and had a slide play of 25mm (1in) to enable it to corner the leading and trailing coupled wheels.

LORD NELSON CLASS 4-6-0

Country of Origin: Great Britain
Railway: Southern Railway (SR)
Date: 1926
Length Overall: 21.279m (69ft 9.75in)
Total Weight: 142,727kg (314,000lb)
Cylinders: 4 419x610mm (16.5x24in)
Driving Wheels: 2.007m (6ft 7in)
Axle Load: 20,909kg (46,000lb)
Fuel: 5,000kg (11,000lb)
Grate Area: 3.1msq (33sq ft)
Water: 22,700lit (5,000gal) (6,000 US gal)
Heating Surface: 185msq (1,989sq ft)
Superheater: 3.5msq (376sq ft)
Steam Pressure: 15.5kg/cmsq (220psi)
Adhesive Weight: 63,181kg (139,000lb)
Tractive Effort: 15,196kg (33,500lb)

No. 850, Lord Nelson, *leaving Appleby in March 1984.*

Only 15 of these magnificent engines were built, because they were difficult to fire and had rather inaccessible mechanisms. They were used throughout the SR network, replacing the King Arthur Class for the heavier loads and holiday expresses.

Country of Origin: USA
Railway: Southern Railway (SR)
Date: 1926
Length Overall: 28.038m (91ft 11.9in)
Total Weight: 255,454kg (562,000lb)
Cylinders: 2 686x711mm (27x28in)
Driving Wheels: 1.854m (6ft 1in)
Axle Load: 27,727kg (61,000lb)
Fuel: 14,545kg (32,000lb)
Grate Area: 6.55msq (70.5sq ft)
Water: 52,664lit (11,600gal) (14,000 US gal)
Heating Surface: 343msq (3,689sq ft)
Superheater: 92.3msq (993sq ft)
Steam Pressure: 14.1kg/cmsq (200psi)
Adhesive Weight: 82,727kg (182,000lb)
Tractive Effort: 21,590kg (47,500lb)

The Class Ps-4 was based on the United States Railroad Administration 4-6-2 heavy-type locomotive design. Initially 36 Class Ps-4 4-6-2s were built in 1923, with a further batch of 23 locomotives following in 1926. Most of these were built by Baldwin and comprised Walschaert's valve gear and mechanical stokers. Southern kept the locomotives in operation into the 1940s, when they were replaced by diesels. The Ps-4s were the last steam passenger locomotives to be ordered and run by the railroad. No. 1401 is on display at the Smithsonian Institution, Washington D.C.

No. 1406 near the end of its working life at Charlottesville in 1947.

ROYAL SCOT CLASS 4-6-0

Country of Origin: Great Britain
Railway: London Midland & Scottish Railway (LMS)
Date: 1927
Length Overall: 19.787m (64ft 11in)
Total Weight: 142,045kg (312,500lb)
Cylinders: 3 457x660mm (18x26in)
Driving Wheels: 2.057m (6ft 9in)
Axle Load: 20,909kg (46,000lb)
Fuel: 9,090kg (20,000lb)
Grate Area: 2.90msq (31.25sq ft)
Water: 18,160lit (4,000gal) (4,800 US gal)
Heating Surface: 172msq (1,851sq ft)
Superheater: 34.1msq (367sq ft)
Steam Pressure: 17.6kg/cmsq (250psi)
Adhesive Weight: 62,272kg (137,000lb)
Tractive Effort: 15,037kg (33,150lb)

No. 6115, Scots Guardsman, *leaving Chinley. This was the last of the class, and was withdrawn from service in 1966.*

A total of 70 Royal Class locomotives were built and when No. 6115, *Scots Guardsman,* ceased running they had seen nearly 40 years of service with London Midland and Scottish. An advanced design in the 1920s, it was influenced by the Lord Nelson Class. They had stepped grates, due to the close spacing of the last pair of wheels, and the single inside cylinder drove the centre wheels. Greater efficiency was achieved by using three independent sets of Walschaert's valve gears.

Country of Origin: USA
Railway: Southern Pacific Railroad (SP)
Date: 1927
Length Overall: 23.99m (78ft 8.5in)
Total Weight: 211,772kg (465,900lb)
Cylinders: 2 558x711mm (22x28in)
Driving Wheels: 2.057m (6ft 9in)
Axle Load: 15,000kg (33,000lb)
Fuel: 11,123lit (2,450gal) (2,940 US gal) oil
Grate Area: 4.6msq (49.5sq ft)
Water: 34,050lit (7,500gal) (9,000 US gal)
Steam Pressure: 14.8kg/cmsq (210psi)
Adhesive Weight: 28,181kg (62,000lb)
Tractive Effort: 18,768kg (41,360lb)

The initial A-6 engines were built at Southern Pacific's workshops in Los Angeles and Sacramento and were virtual rebuilds of early Baldwin and Alco A-3 engines which had already seen more than 20 years' service. The rebuilt locomotives were fitted with booster engines which drove the rear wheels and Walschaert's valve gears. A pair of locomotives were specially painted in orange and black livery and designed for the prestigious daylight express that operated between Los Angeles and San Francisco, California.

No. 3025 was the last Atlantic in service and had the honour to haul President Roosevelt's presidential tour train.

KING CLASS 4-6-0

Country of Origin: Great Britain
Railway: Great Western Railway
Date: 1927
Length Overall: 20.777m (68ft 2in)
Total Weight: 138,181kg (304,000lb)
Cylinders: 4 413x711mm (16.25x28in)
Driving Wheels: 1.981m (6ft 6in)
Axle Load: 22,954kg (50,500lb)
Fuel: 6,136kg (13,500lb)
Grate Area: 3.19msq (343sq ft)
Water: 18,160lit (4,000gal) (4,800 US gal)
Heating Surface: 204msq (2,201sq ft)
Superheater: 29.0msq (313sq ft)
Steam Pressure: 17.6kg/cmsq (250psi)
Adhesive Weight: 68,636kg (151,000lb)
Tractive Effort: 18,285kg (40,300lb)

The King George V was the most powerful 4-6-0 in Great Britain and is now preserved in Hereford.

First came the Star Class locomotives, then the Castles, and finally the Kings: each a stretched version of the other and each more powerful than its predecessor. The King Class was derived from the de Glehn arrangement, with the outside cylinders driving the coupled axle and the inside pair driving the leading axle. Walschaert's valve gear was used, positioned inside the frames. In all, 30 King Class locomotives were built. The first batch of six entered service in 1927 and the last of the class was withdrawn from service in 1962. The locomotives were named in reverse chronological order from the then monarch, King George V. The King Class 4-6-0 locomotives proved to be a great success for the Great Western Railway.

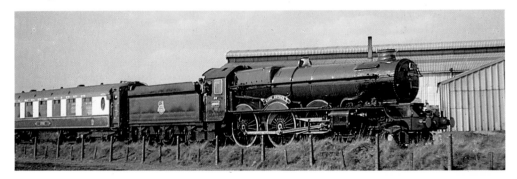

AC-4 CAB FORWARD 4-8-8-2

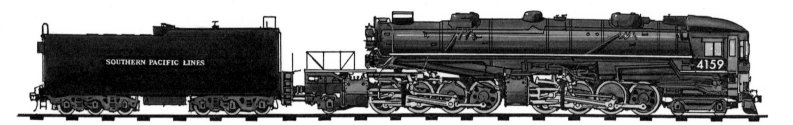

Country of Origin: USA
Railway: Southern Pacific Railroad (SP)
Date: 1928
Length Overall: 38.075m (124ft 11in)
Total Weight: 477,818kg (1,051,200lb)
Cylinders: 4 609x812mm (24x32in)
Driving Wheels: 1.61m (5ft 3.5in)
Axle Load: 31,800kg (69,960lb)
Fuel: 23,076lit (5,083gal) (6,100 US gal)
Grate Area: 12.9msq (139sq ft)
Water: 83,232lit (18,333gal) (22,000 US gal)
Heating Surface: 601msq (6,470sq ft)
Superheater: 243msq (2,616sq ft)
Steam Pressure: 17.6kg/cmsq (250psi)
Adhesive Weight: 241,682kg (531,700lb)
Tractive Effort: 56,397kg (124,300lb)

The AC-4 locomotives were extremely heavy, weighing almost as much as the huge Union Pacific Big Boys of the 1940s, and these oil-fuelled locomotives were consequently rather slow with maximum speeds of only 89km/h (55mph). These cab-forward locomotives, of which 243 were built in total for Southern Pacific, were therefore relegated to freight trains.

The first cab-forward entered service in 1911 when 12 2-6-6-2 engines were built. These were later converted to 4-6-6-2s and a further 36 were built during the next two years, with another alteration in wheel arrangement to 2-8-8-2. These were known as Mallet-Consolidations and carried the designations of MC-2, MC-4, and MC-6. The first articulated consolidation locomotives, designated AC-4s, were built by Baldwin between 1928 and 1944. Eventually, all of the MC Class cab-forwards were converted to AC Class locomotives.

Baldwin's works photograph of the front view of No. 4159, built by them for Southern Pacific. These were the most successful cab-in-front locomotives ever built.

SCHOOLS CLASS 4-4-0

Country of Origin: Great Britain
Railway: Southern Railway (SR)
Date: 1930
Length Overall: 17.926m (58ft 9.75in)
Total Weight: 111,591kg (245,800lb)
Cylinders: 3 419x660mm (16.5x26in)
Driving Wheels: 2.007m (6ft 7in)
Axle Load: 21,363kg (47,000lb)
Fuel: 5,000kg (11,000lb)
Grate Area: 2.63msq (28.3sq ft)
Water: 18,160lit (4,000gal) (4,800 US gal)
Heating Surface: 164msq (1,766sq ft)
Superheater: 26.3msq (283sq ft)
Steam Pressure: 15.46kg/cmsq (220psi)
Adhesive Weight: 42,727kg (94,000lb)
Tractive Effort: 11,400kg (25,133lb)

No. 928, Slough, at Cranmore. This is one of three that have been preserved after they were withdrawn from service in 1962.

Between 1930 and 1935 40 School Class locomotives were built. First of Class No. 900, *Eton*, was from the initial batch of 10, all built at Eastleigh Works.

Country of Origin: Ireland
Railway: Great Northern Railway (GNR(I))
Date: 1932
Length Overall: 16.853m (55ft 3.5in)
Total Weight: 105,454kg (232,000lb)
Cylinders: HP: 1 438x660mm (17.25x26in);
LP: 2 483x660mm (19x26in)
Driving Wheels: 2.007m (6ft 7in)
Axle Load: 21,363kg (47,000lb)
Fuel: 6,000kg (13,200lb)
Grate Area: 2.3msq (25sq ft)
Water: 15,840lit (3,500gal) (4,200 US gal)
Heating Surface: 116msq (1,251sq ft)
Superheater: 25.6msq (278sq ft)
Steam Pressure: 17.6kg/cmsq (250psi)
Adhesive Weight: 41,818kg (92,000lb)

No. 85, Merlin, *is here shown on a passenger excursion.*

The first of the heavier, more powerful Irish locomotives of the 1930s. The Beyer, Peacock-built Class V compounds featured Stephenson's link motion and piston valves on all cylinders. They established a running time from Dublin to Belfast of 2hrs 28mins over a much improved track. This included the border stop and five refuelling stops. The last Class V 4-4-0s were retired from service in 1961.

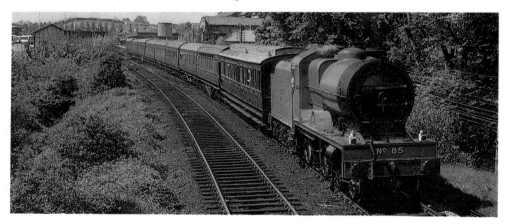

KF TYPE 4-8-4

Country of Origin: China
Railway: Chinese Ministry of Railways
Date: 1935
Length Overall: 28.41m (93ft 2.5in)
Total Weight: 196,363kg (432,000lb)
Cylinders: 2 540x750mm (21.25x29.5in)
Driving Wheels: 1.75m (5ft 9in)
Axle Load: 17,272kg (38,000lb)
Fuel: 12,045kg (26,500lb)
Grate Area: 6.4msq (68.5sq ft)
Water: 29,964lit (6,600gal) (8,000 US gal)
Heating Surface: 278msq (2,988sq ft)
Superheater: 100msq (1,076sq ft)
Steam Pressure: 15.5kg/cmsq (220psi)
Adhesive Weight: 68,181kg (150,000lb)
Tractive Effort: 16,380kg (36,100lb)

Built by the Vulcan Foundry in Newton-le-Willows, Lancashire. KF Class No. 7 stands in Shanghai just prior to being returned to the National Railway Museum, York in 1981.

Operating on the Canton-Hanken and the Shanghai-Nanking Railways, 24 KF Type 4-8-4s were built in Great Britain. The locomotives, which featured automatic stokers, valve gear setting indicators and electric lights in the cabs, remained in service until the 1960s. All engines had Walschaert valve gear and many had the benefit of a booster engine fitted to the leading tender bogie. No. KF7 was returned to the National Railway Museum in York in 1981 by the Chinese People's Republic.

Country of Origin: Peru
Railway: Central Railway of Peru (FCC)
Date: 1935
Length Overall: 18.879m (61ft 11.25in)
Total Weight: 113,636kg (250,000lb)
Cylinders: 2 508x711mm (20x28in)
Driving Wheels: 1.321m (4ft 4in)
Axle Load: 16,591kg (36,500lb)
Fuel: 6,656lit (1,465gal) (1,760 US gal) oil
Grate Area: 2.6msq (28sq ft)
Water: 12,031lit (2,650gal) (3,1800 US gal)
Heating Surface: 160msq (1,717sq ft)
Superheater: 32msq (341sq ft)
Steam Pressure: 14.1kg/cmsq (200psi)
Adhesive Weight: 66,364kg (146,000lb)
Tractive Effort: 16,600kg (36,600lb)

These extremely hard-working, robust engines achieved only 14.1kg/cm sq (200psi) of steam pressure which was due partly to their larger-than-necessary cylinders and partly to their being fuelled by oil.

Beyer, Peacock built 29 locomotives which were supplied to the Central Railway of Peru; a further five were supplied to the Cerro de Pasco Railroad, and another 20 to the Southern Railway of Peru. In order to tackle the steep gradients encountered, especially on the Lima—Gallera Line, which climbed 4,750m (15,750ft) in less than 150km (93 miles), they were all fitted with shortened boilers. They also featured air sanding to increase their track adhesion and a very complicated air-braking system. They benefited from having to pull only a small tender, since there were plentiful supplies of water en route. Only one locomotive has been preserved, No. 206, which is exhibited at the Lima Railway Museum.

An oil-burning Baldwin Andes Class locomotive leaves Machu Pichu Station, Peru with the passenger train to Cuzco.

CLASS A 4-4-2

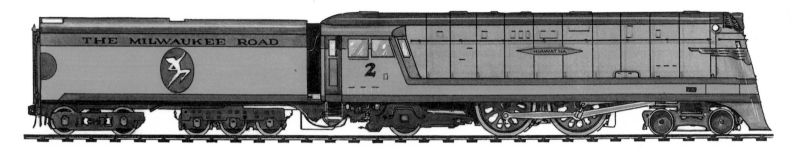

Country of Origin: USA
Railway: Chicago, Milwaukee, St. Paul & Pacific Railroad (CMStP&P)
Date: 1935
Length Overall: 27.026m (88ft 8in)
Total Weight: 244,091kg (537,000lb)
Cylinders: 2 483x711mm (19x28in)
Driving Wheels: 2.483m (7ft)
Axle Load: 32,955kg (72,500lb)
Fuel: 14,982lit (3,300gal) (4,000 US gal)
Grate Area: 6.4msq (69sq ft)
Water: 49,032lit (10,800gal) (13,000 US gal)
Heating Surface: 301.5msq (3,245sq ft)
Superheater: 96msq (1,029sq ft)
Steam Pressure: 21kg/cmsq (300psi)
Adhesive Weight: 65,682kg (144,500lb)
Tractive Effort: 13,920kg (30,685lb)

Class A 4-4-2 No. 1, with a 5-coach luxury Chippewa train, near Deerfield, Illinois in 1939.

Alco (the American Locomotive Company) of Schenectady, New York, built only four streamlined Class A locomotives in the bright livery of the Chicago, Milwaukee, St Paul and Pacific Railroad. The locomotives were purposely built for daily 177km/h (110mph) service on the luxury Hiawatha trains running from Chicago to St Paul and Minneapolis. The Hiawatha train had nine cars for the longer journey.

Country of Origin: Great Britain
Railway: London & North Eastern Railway (LNER)
Date: 1935
Length Overall: 21.64m (71ft)
Total Weight: 167,795kg (370,000lb)
Cylinders: 3 470x660mm (18.5x26in)
Driving Wheels: 2,032m (6ft 8in)
Axle Load: 22,448kg (49,500lb)
Fuel: 8,163kg (18,000lb)
Grate Area: 3.8msq (41sq ft)
Water: 22,717lit (5,000gal) (6,000 US gal)
Heating Surface: 240msq (2,576sq ft)
Superheater: 70msq (749sq ft)
Steam Pressure: 17.5kg/cmsq (250psi)
Adhesive Weight: 67,118kg (148,000lb)
Tractive Effort: 16,086kg (35,455lb)

No. 4498, Sir Nigel Gresley, *ascends the Settle–Carlisle line.*

On 4 July 1938 No. 4468, *Mallard*, broke the World Steam Traction speed record with a sustained speed of 201km/h (125mph). Three years earlier, on 27 September 1935, the first of four streamlined locomotives, No. 2509 (*Silver Link*), had also broken the speed record when it achieved 180km/h (112.5mph) on its press trip.

The A4 Class 4-6-2 is a direct descendant of the Class A1 *Flying Scotsman* and was designed specifically to run between London and Newcastle, a distance of 429km (268 miles). The first locomotive entered service as the Silver Jubilee train on 30 September 1935 to immediate acclaim. The A4 Class was probably the best steam locomotive ever to be built and one of the most popular. A total of 32 A4s were built in two years.

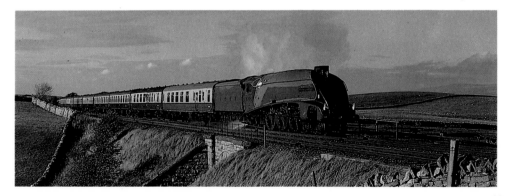

CLASS 05 4-6-4

Country of Origin: Germany
Railway: German State Railway (DR)
Date: 1935
Length Overall: 26.265m (86ft 2in)
Total Weight: 215,938kg (475,064lb)
Cylinders: 3 450x660mm (17.75x26in)
Driving Wheels: 2.3m (7ft 6.5in)
Axle Load: 19,545kg (43,000lb)
Fuel: 10,000kg (22,000lb)
Grate Area: 4.71msq (51sq ft)
Water: 37,228lit (8,200gal) (9,870 US gal)
Heating Surface: 256msq (2,750sq ft)
Superheater: 90msq (976sq ft)
Steam Pressure: 20kg/cmsq (284psi)
Adhesive Weight: 57,727kg (127,000lb)
Tractive Effort: 14,870kg (32,776lb)

No. 05001 is an exhibit at the Nuremberg National Railway Museum. Here it is shown breaking the steam speed record in March 1935.

Only three Class 05 locomotives were built by Börsig of Berlin. Partially streamlined, they were designed to run at an operating speed of 150km/h (94mph) which at the time was faster than any other European steam train. No. 05001 has been restored.

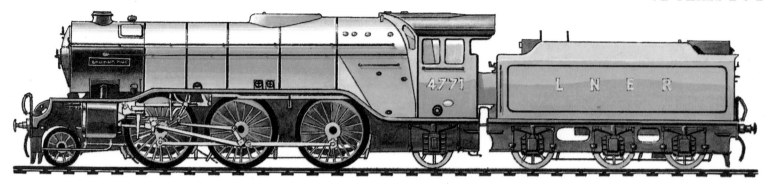

Country of Origin: Great Britain
Railway: London & North Eastern Railway (LNER)
Date: 1936
Length Overall: 20.244m (66ft 5in)
Total Weight: 146,818kg (323,000lb)
Cylinders: 3 470x660mm (18.5x26in)
Driving Wheels: 1.88m (6ft 2in)
Axle Load: 22,500kg (49,500lb)
Fuel: 7,727kg (17,000lb)
Grate Area: 3.86msq (41.25sq ft)
Water: 19,068lit (4,200gal) (5,040 US gal)
Heating Surface: 225.8msq (2,431sq ft)
Superheater: 63.2msq (680sq ft)
Steam Pressure: 15.5kg/cmsq (220psi)
Adhesive Weight: 66,364kg (146,000lb)
Tractive Effort: 15,304kg (33,730lb)

No. 4771, Green Arrow, on a special steam excursion in the Hope Valley.

A total of 184 V2 Class 2-6-2 Green Arrows were built and remained in service for 30 years until 1966 and, of these, No. 4771 *Green Arrow* has been preserved in working condition at the National Railway Museum, York, and is also illustrated here, passing through Hope Valley. Although originally intended for fast fitted freights, they proved to be such an equal match for the A3 Pacifics that they gained work on the prestigious Yorkshire Pullman as early as 1939. During the Second World War these reliable engines provided outstanding duty: such performances never went unnoticed, including a journey made by No. 4800 from Peterborough to King's Cross, all in 26 coaches with a gross load weight of some 873,815kg (1,922,393lb) in 102 minutes. This performance was more than double what the engine was designed for.

231-132BT CLASS 4-6-2 + 2-6-4

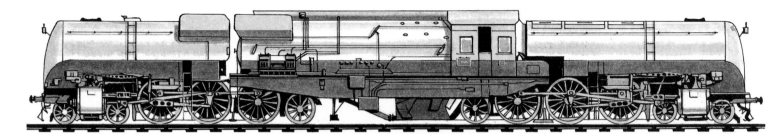

Country of Origin: Algeria
Railway: Paris, Lyons & Mediterranean
Railway (PLM)
Date: 1937
Length Overall: 29.432m (96ft 6.8in)
Total Weight: 21,591kg (47,500lb)
Cylinders: 4 490x660mm (19.25x26in)
Driving Wheels: 1.8m (5ft 11in)
Axle Load: 18,409kg (40,500lb)
Fuel: 10,909kg (24,000lb)
Grate Area: 5.4msq (58sq ft)
Water: 29,964lit (6,600gal) (7,900 US gal)
Heating Surface: 260msq (2,794sq ft)
Superheater: 91msq (975sq ft)
Steam Pressure: 20kg/cmsq (284psi)
Adhesive Weight: 109,545kg (241,000lb)
Tractive Effort: 29,920kg (65,960lb)

*Double-headed Garratts on the
Pietermaritzburg–Greytown line haul 720
tonnes out of Albert Falls up a 1-in-30
gradient.*

These strange-looking Beyer-Garratts were
built by Raismes in France. They were
originally ordered by the Paris, Lyons &
Mediterranean Company, who first ordered
10 and then a further 19 locomotives after
they amalgamated with the Algerian State
railways to become Algerian railways. The
231-132BT Class locomotives remained in
service until 1957; after that date many
Beyer-Garratts remained in operation in
Southern Africa. Cabs were fitted with
duplicate controls at the rear of the cab for
reverse running and the locomotives had
electrically-operated Cossart valve gear,
which drove cam-operated piston valves.

Country of Origin: Canada
Railway: Canadian Pacific Railway (CPR)
Date: 1937
Length Overall: 27.686m (90ft 10in)
Total Weight: 299,545kg (659,000lb)
Cylinders: 2 559x762mm (22x30in)
Driving Wheels: 1.905m (6ft 3in)
Axle Load: 29,545kg (65,000lb)
Fuel: 21,364kg (47,000lb)
Grate Area: 7.5msq (81sq ft)
Water: 54,480lit (12,000gal) (14,400 US gal)
Heating Surface: 352msq (3,791sq ft)
Superheater: 143msq (1,542sq ft)
Steam Pressure: 19.3kg/cmsq (275psi)
Adhesive Weight: 88,162kg (194,000lb)
Tractive Effort: 20,548kg (45,300lb)

All 45 of the Royal Hudson Class locomotives that were built featured mechanical stokers and large superheaters with front-end throttles fitted to their sides. In 1939 No. 2850 hauled the royal train of King George VI and Queen Elizabeth on their lengthy visit to Canada, since which time a crown has been painted at the front of the running board.

With a production life spanning the nine years from 1937 to 1945, this class, originally designated Class H-1, remained in service with the Canadian Pacific Railway until 1966.

No. 2860 at Montreal Locomotive Works in 1982. This is one of five surviving locomotives and is used for hauling tourist trains on the British Columbia Railway from Vancouver to Squamish.

CLASS J3a 4-6-4

Country of Origin: USA
Railway: New York Central Railroad (NYC)
Date: 1937
Length Overall: 32.342m (106ft 1in)
Total Weight: 354,545kg (780,000lb)
Cylinders: 2 527x737mm (22.5x29in)
Driving Wheels: 2.007m (6ft 7in)
Axle Load: 30,681kg (67,500lb)
Fuel: 41,818kg (92,000lb)
Grate Area: 7.6msq (82sq ft)
Water: 68,100lit (15,000gal) (18,000 US gal)
Heating Surface: 389msq (4,187sq ft)
Superheater: 162.1msq (1,745sq ft)
Steam Pressure: 18.6kg/cmsq (265psi)
Adhesive Weight: 91,590kg (201,500lb)
Tractive Effort: 19,000kg (41,860lb)

No. 5280, a Class J1 4-6-4, is depicted hauling the Empire State Express at Dunkirk in February 1950. This was the direct ancestor of the J3a.

The Class J3a Hudsons built by Alco were the direct descendants of the Class J1a which first entered service in 1926, then the first 4-6-4s in the United States. The Class was finally taken out of service in 1956, although many had been replaced earlier by the Niagara Class 4-8-4s. The New York Central Railroad had the largest fleet of 4-6-4 locomotives, which included 275 J3s used to haul the prestigious Twentieth Century Limited train from New York to Chicago in only 16 hours.

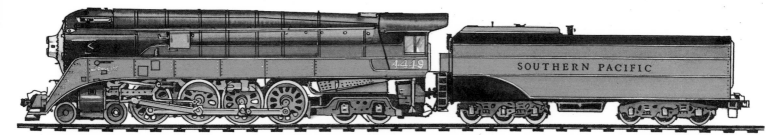

Country of Origin: USA
Railway: Southern Pacific Railroad (SP)
Date: 1937
Length Overall: 30.91m (101ft 5in)
Total Weight: 401,364kg (883,000lb)
Cylinders: 2 648x813mm (25.5x32in)
Driving Wheels: 1.87m (6ft 1.5in)
Axle Load: 31,330kg (68,925lb)
Fuel: 22,263lit (4,900gal) (5,900 US gal) oil
Grate Area: 8.4msq (90.4sq ft)
Water: 88,984lit (19,600gal) (23,500 US gal)
Heating Surface: 454msq (4,887sq ft)
Superheater: 194msq (2,086sq ft)
Steam Pressure: 21.1kg/cmsq (300psi)
Adhesive Weight: 125,455kg (276,000lb)
Tractive Effort: 32,285kg (71,173lb)

Streamlined and brightly coloured, the GS-2 locomotives pulled the Daylight Express complete with its 12 matching cars from Los Angeles to San Francisco. Built by the Lima Locomotive works in Ohio, they remained in service for 20 years. A total of some 60 locomotives were built, although the first batch of six had smaller driving wheels and were designated GS-2 when they entered service in 1937. No. 4460 has been preserved and is now at the Museum of Transportation, St Louis, Missouri.

Features included electro-pneumatic braking equipment, spring-controlled side-play on the leading coupled axle, air sanding gear and three turbo-generators, and a feed-water heater and pump which were in addition to injectors.

Southern Pacific's Daylight Express was one of the early luxury streamliners serving San Francisco and Los Angeles and built its reputation on speed and service.

CLASS 56 4-6-2

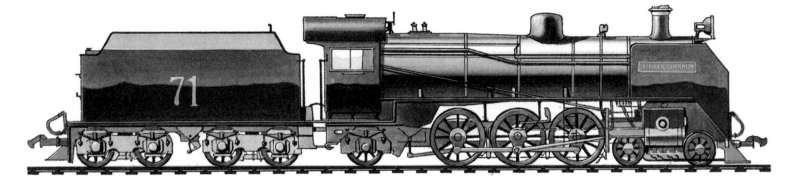

Country of Origin: Malaysia
Railway: Malayan Railway (PKTM)
Date: 1938
Length Overall: 18.628m (61ft 1.4in)
Total Weight: 102,727kg (226,000lb)
Cylinders: 3 330x610mm (13x24in)
Driving Wheels: 1.372m (4ft 6in)
Axle Load: 12,982kg (28,560lb)
Fuel: 10,000kg (22,000lb)
Grate Area: 2.5msq (27sq ft)
Water: 15,890lit (3,500gal) (4,200 US gal)
Heating Surface: 103msq (1,109sq ft)
Superheater: 20.25msq (218sq ft)
Steam Pressure: 17.5kg/cmsq (250psi)
Adhesive Weight: 39,091kg (86,000lb)
Tractive Effort: 10,859kg (23,940lb)

Originally designated Class 'O', 68 of these three-cylindered locomotives were built by the North British Locomotive Company for

use on the metre-gauge tracks of the Malaysian Railway (formerly the Federated Malaya State Railway). Each locomotive was uniquely named, with the name displayed in Roman script on one side of the engine and in Malay script on the other. Originally coal burning, all engines were converted to oil in 1955, just before their demise with the introduction of diesels in 1957. They were, however, in limited use right up until 1981. These very light locomotives weighed only 102,727kg (226,000lb) and were restricted to a speed limit of 72.5km/h (45mph) over what was indifferent, lightly laid track.

No. 56436, Temerloh, departs Kuala Lumpur with a private excursion train to Batu Caves in September 1964.

Country of Origin: Great Britain
Railway: London, Midland & Scottish Railway (LMS)
Date: 1939
Length Overall: 22.51m (73ft 10.25in)
Total Weight: 164,545kg (362,000lb)
Cylinders: 4 419x711mm (16.5x28in)
Driving Wheels: 2.057m (6ft 9in)
Axle Load: 23,864kg (52,500lb)
Fuel: 10,182kg (22,400lb)
Grate Area: 4.6msq (50sq ft)
Water: 18,160lit (4,000gal) (4,800 US gal)
Heating Surface: 261msq (2,807sq ft)
Superheater: 79.5msq (856sq ft)
Steam Pressure: 17.6kg/cmsq (250psi)
Adhesive Weight: 67,045kg (147,500lb)
Tractive Effort: 18,144kg (40,000lb)

No. 46229, the Duchess of Hamilton, *which has been preserved at the National Railway Museum. Two other locomotives of the class are also preserved.*

The Duchess Class 4-6-2 were the most powerful steam locomotives ever to be run in Great Britain and in February 1939 recorded an indicated horsepower of 3,300 during a run from Glasgow to Crewe in which two firemen were employed. The Duchess Class locomotives were designed by William Stanier and incorporated outside valve gear which connected to the valves on both the inside and outside of the cylinders via rocker arms behind the outside cylinders. A total of 38 Duchess Class locomotives were built and remained in service from 1939 through to 1964.

CLASS 12 4-4-2

Country of Origin: Belgium
Railway: Belgium National Railways (SNCB)
Date: 1939
Length Overall: 21.19m (69ft 6.25in)
Total Weight: 85,682kg (188,500lb)
Cylinders: 2 480x720mm (18.8x28.4in)
Driving Wheels: 2.1m (6ft 10.75in)
Axle Load: 23,636kg (52,000lb)
Fuel: 7,955kg (17,500lb)
Grate Area: 3.7msq (39.8sq ft)
Water: 23,971lit (5,280gal) (6,300 US gal)
Heating Surface: 161msq (1,729sq ft)
Superheater: 63msq (678sq ft)
Steam Pressure: 18kg/cmsq (256psi)
Adhesive Weight: 45,909kg (101,000lb)
Tractive Effort: 12,079kg (26,620lb)

Built by Cockrill in Belgium, these were the last 4-4-2 steam locomotives to be built anywhere in the world and their working life was cut short by the war. They were designed specifically for the 120km (75 miles) run from Brussels to Ostend.

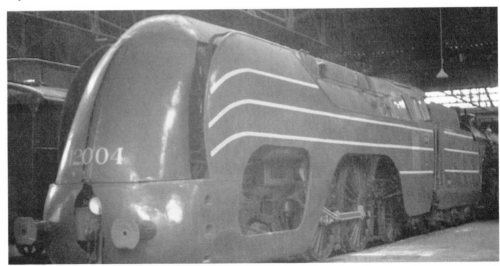

No. 12004 is one of the world's last 4-4-2s.

Country of Origin: USA
Railway: Norfolk & Western Railway (N&W)
Date: 1941
Length Overall: 30.759m (100ft 11in)
Total Weight: 396,818kg (873,000lb)
Cylinders: 2 686x813mm (27x32in)
Driving Wheels: 1.778m (5ft 10in)
Axle Load: 32,727kg (72,000lb)
Fuel: 31,818kg (70,000lb)
Grate Area: 10msq (107.5sq ft)
Water: 75,818lit (16,700gal) (20,000 US gal)
Heating Surface: 490msq (5,271sq ft)
Superheater: 202msq (2,177sq ft)
Steam Pressure: 21kg/cmsq (300psi)
Adhesive Weight: 130,909kg (288,000lb)
Tractive Effort: 36,287kg (80,000lb)

One of the most efficient locomotives ever was built by Norfolk and Western at their Roanoke, Virginia works. The Class J 4-8-4 engines only required visits to the workshops every 18 months, during which time they had travelled on average some 24,000km (15,000 miles). In addition to that their regular services, which involved cleaning and oil change, took only one hour. The result was that the Norfolk and Western quickly became the most efficient and profitable railroad in North America. The locomotive frame was made of cast steel and featured a multitude of automatically oiled bearings. For this purpose a huge oil tank of 110lit (29 gal) was fitted. Other features were Baker's valve gear and an enormous fender.

No. 611 was built at Roanoke in 1950, one of the last batch of three mainline passenger locomotives ever to be built in the United States.

BIG BOY 4-8-8-4

Country of Origin: USA
Railway: Union Pacific Railroad (UP)
Date: 1941
Length Overall: 40.487m (132ft 10in)
Total Weight: 540,682kg (1,189,500lb)
Cylinders: 4 603x812mm (23.75x32in)
Driving Wheels: 1.727m (5ft 8in)
Axle Load: 30,795kg (67,750lb)
Fuel: 25,455kg (56,000lb)
Grate Area: 13.9msq (150sq ft)
Water: 94,500lit (20,800gal) (25,000 US gal)
Heating Surface: 547msq (5,889sq ft)
Superheater: 229msq (2,466sq ft)
Steam Pressure: 21.1kg/cmsq (300psi)
Adhesive Weight: 245,455kg (540,000lb)
Tractive Effort: 61,422kg (135,375lb)

Union Pacific's Big Boy *is currently on display at Steamtown, Bellows Falls, Vermont.*

The very epitome of everything big, powerful and enviable in American railroading, these Union Pacific (UP) 4-8-8-4 locomotives created an unsurpassed reputation for themselves. The first 4-cylinder giant entered service in September 1941 and immediately UP had to relay heavier track to cope with their 6,000 ton trains and build new turntables to manage their 40m (132ft) length. The were built with cast-steel frames, and comfortably attained speeds of 112km/h (70mph). Of the 201 Big Boy locomotives built, six have been preserved, although none of these is in working order.

Country of Origin: USA
Railway: Chesapeake & Ohio Railroad (Chessie)
Date: 1941
Length Overall: 39.653m (130ft 1in)
Total Weight: 489,091kg (1,076,000lb)
Cylinders: 4 571x838mm (22.5x33in)
Driving Wheels: 1.701m (5ft 7in)
Axle Load: 39,250kg (86,350lb)
Fuel: 22,727kg (50,000lb)
Grate Area: 12.5msq (135sq ft)
Water: 94,500lit (20,800gal) (25,000 US gal)
Heating Surface: 673msq (7,240sq ft)
Superheater: 296msq (3,186sq ft)
Steam Pressure: 18.3kg/cmsq (260psi)
Adhesive Weight: 214,091kg (471,000lb)
Tractive Effort: 80,000kg (110,200lb)

Allegheny No. 1648 takes on water at Russell, Kentucky in May 1949.

Allegheny 2-6-6-6 locomotives were built by the Lima Locomotive Works, of which 60 were delivered to the Chesapeake and Ohio Railway with the remaining eight going to the Virginia Railroad. Designed to haul the massive coal trains, they were the most powerful engines ever built and were capable, when working in tandem, of moving 140 coal cars (which totalled 11,500 tonnes) up the long climb from Hinton to the summit of the Allegheny mountains. Their working life was short due to the advent of the diesels, and by 1956 all had been withdrawn from service. At one stage or another 20 of them had also been used for passenger work in addition to their coal-hauling duties. Features included Baker's valve gear, Worthington feed-water heaters and roller bearings on all axles. No. 1604 is on exhibition in Roanoke, Virginia.

CHALLENGER CLASS 4-6-6-4

Country of Origin: USA
Railway: Union Pacific Railroad (UP)
Date: 1942
Length Overall: 37.16m (121ft 11in)
Total Weight: 486,818kg (1,071,000lb)
Cylinders: 4 533x813mm (21x32in)
Driving Wheels: 1.753m (5ft 7in)
Axle Load: 30,909kg (68,000lb)
Fuel: 25,455kg (56,000lb)
Grate Area: 12.3msq (132sq ft)
Water: 94,500lit (20,800gal) (25,000 US gal)
Heating Surface: 431msq (4,642sq ft)
Superheater: 162msq (1,741sq ft)
Steam Pressure: 19.7kg/cmsq (280psi)
Adhesive Weight: 184,545kg (406,000lb)
Tractive Effort: 44,100kg (97,400lb)

The Challenger Class locomotives were introduced experimentally in 1942 for passenger work and were based on a successful freight locomotive, of which Union Pacific operated 34. Alterations were made after the first batch of six and 65 of the improved version entered service in 1944. Weighing in at one million pounds, they were the heaviest, largest and most powerful articulated passenger locomotives ever built. They featured smaller boilers than their freight predecessors but with a higher pressure, cast-steel frames and a vertical hinge only between the main frame and the leading unit, the horizontal hinge being compensated for by the fitting of springs to each axle. By 1958 all had been withdrawn from service but No. 3985 has been restored and it may now be seen in working condition at Cheyenne, Wyoming.

Union Pacific's Challenger Class were the most powerful locomotives ever designed for passenger work. Here No. 3985 passes through Laramie.

Country of Origin: USA
Railway: Northern Pacific Railroad (NP)
Date: 1943
Length Overall: 34.391m (112ft 10in)
Total Weight: 432,727kg (952,000lb)
Cylinders: 2 711x762mm (28x30in)
Driving Wheels: 1.956m (6ft 5in)
Axle Load: 33,636kg (74,000lb)
Fuel: 24,545kg (54,000lb)
Grate Area: 10.7msq (115sq ft)
Water: 95,340lit (21,000gal) (12,000 US gal)
Heating Surface: 433msq (4,660sq ft)
Superheater: 185msq (1,992sq ft)
Steam Pressure: 18.3kg/cmsq (260psi)
Adhesive Weight: 13,409kg (295,000lb)
Tractive Effort: 31,660kg (69,800lb)

The first Class A 4-8-4 locomotives in North America entered service in 1927 with the Canadian National Railway and saw service with 39 railway companies. One of those was Northern Pacific which from then on never ordered a different wheel combination for any passenger work, but developed and refined the 4-8-4. The A-5 was their final order, some 30 per cent heavier than the original A-1s which had been built by the American Locomotive Company (Alco). Northern Pacific's total order over the years was for 12 original Class A locomotives, 10 A-2s in 1934, 8 A-3s in 1938, 8 A-4s in 1941 and 10 A-5s, all of which – after the A-1s – were built by Baldwin. The Class A-5 locomotives hold the world steam record for a journey of 1,608km (999 miles) from St Paul to Livingstone, Montana, without an engine change.

A-3 No. 2664 hauls freight past Manitoba Junction, Minnesota.

CLASS UL-F 4-8-2

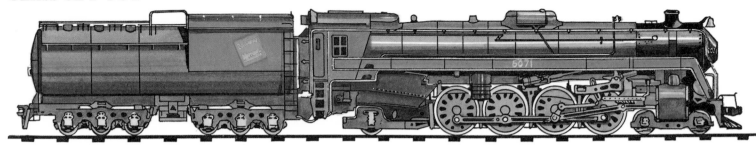

Country of Origin: Canada
Railway: Canadian National Railways (CNR)
Date: 1944
Length Overall: 28.426m (93ft 3in)
Total Weight: 290,000kg (638,000lb)
Cylinders: 2 610x762mm (24x30in)
Driving Wheels: 1.854m (6ft 1in)
Axle Load: 27,045kg (59,500lb)
Fuel: 18,182kg (40,000lb)
Grate Area: 6.6msq (70.2sq ft)
Water: 52,210lit (11,500gal) (13,800 US gal)
Heating Surface: 333msq (3,584sq ft)
Superheater: 146msq (1,570sq ft)
Steam Pressure: 18.3kg/cmsq (260psi)
Adhesive Weight: 107,727kg (237,000lb)
Tractive Effort: 23,814kg (52,500lb)

These impressive-looking locomotives sported side valences, a Bristol-style smoke stack that was flanged, brass number plates and Vanderbilt cylindrical tenders.

The original Class UL locomotives entered service in 1923, and these eight-coupled locomotives were eventually developed and refined into the 1944 UL-F 4-8-2 for Canadian National Railways. CNR have successfully preserved six engines in working condition, which feature cast-steel frames and exhaust steam injectors.

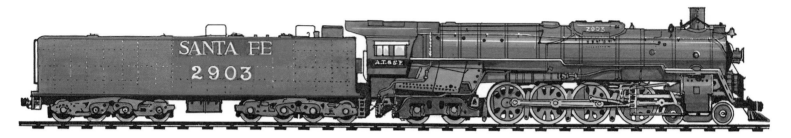

Country of Origin: USA
Railway: Atchison, Topeka & Santa Fe Railway (AT & SF)
Date: 1944
Length Overall: 36.830m (120ft 10in)
Total Weight: 436,818kg (961,000lb)
Cylinders: 2 711x813mm (28x32in)
Driving Wheels: 2.032m (6ft 8in)
Axle Load: 33,636kg (74,000lb)
Fuel: 26,488lit (5,830gal) (7,000 US gal)
Grate Area: 10msq (108sq ft)
Water: 92,616lit (20,400gal) (24,500 US gal)
Heating Surface: 494msq (5,313sq ft)
Superheater: 220msq (2,366sq ft)
Steam Pressure: 21kg/cmsq (300psi)
Adhesive Weight: 133,636kg (294,000lb)
Tractive Effort: 36,270kg (79,960lb)

This 4-8-4 is preserved at Albuquerque, New Mexico, although not in working condition.

Santa-Fe rostered these locomotives, of which they had 65, to run straight through without locomotive change from Kansas City to Los Angeles via the Raton Pass, a distance of 2,830km (1,760 miles) and the longest distance ever rostered in such a way. They scheduled the 34 hour trip with 12 crew changes, 12 fuel stops and 16 water stops. Unfortunately none has been preserved in working condition, though No. 2903 is on show in Chicago. The 2900 Class 4-8-4s were the largest straight (non-articulated) steam passenger locomotives ever built and also the heaviest.

FEF-3 CLASS 4-8-4

Country of Origin: USA
Railway: Union Pacific Railroad (UP)
Date: 1944
Length Overall: 34.696m (113ft 10in)
Total Weight: 412,727kg (908,000lb)
Cylinders: 2 635x813mm (25x32in)
Driving Wheels: 2.032m (6ft 8in)
Axle Load: 30,455kg (67,000lb)
Fuel: 22,727kg (50,000lb)
Grate Area: 9.3msq (100sq ft)
Water: 89,052lit (19,600gal) (23,500 US gal)
Heating Surface: 393msq (4,225sq ft)
Superheater: 130msq (1,400sq ft)
Steam Pressure: 21kg/cmsq (300psi)
Adhesive Weight: 121,136kg (266,500lb)
Tractive Effort: 28,950kg (63,800lb)

Another of the North American locomotives that was progressively developed over the years, the FEF class first entered service in 1938 when 20 FEF-1 engines with 12-wheeled tenders were ordered by Union Pacific. In 1939 15 FEF-2 locomotives followed and a final batch of ten were designated FED-3 in 1944.

This last batch was converted to oil-burning soon after entering service, and was eventually withdrawn from service in 1959. They featured cast-steel frames and a static exhaust steam injector both to drive the water pump and feed the water heater.

No. 8444 passes through La Salle, Colorado on an excursion from Denver to Sterling, Colorado.

Country of Origin: USA
Railway: New York Central Railroad (NYC)
Date: 1945
Length Overall: 35.192m (115ft 5.5in)
Total Weight: 405,000kg (891,000lb)
Cylinders: 2 648x813mm (25.5x32in)
Driving Wheels: 2.007m (6ft 7in)
Axle Load: 31,818kg (70,000lb)
Fuel: 41,818kg (92,000lb)
Grate Area: 9.3msq (100sq ft)
Water: 68,100lit (15,000gal) (18,000 US gal)
Heating Surface: 4.48msq (4,827sq ft)
Superheater: 191msq (2,060sq ft)
Steam Pressure: 19.3kg/cmsq (275psi)
Adhesive Weight: 124,545kg (274,000lb)
Tractive Effort: 27,936kg (61,570lb)

The first of its Class, No. 6001, leaves Albany, New York heading south, 1952.

The American Locomotive Company (Alco) built 25 Niagara Class 4-8-4 locomotives in addition to a prototype and an experimental engine. They were designed for operation on the New York–Chicago line, and were scheduled to make the journey in 16 hours including one stop for refuelling. They took on water with a pick-up scoop while travelling at 128km/h (80mph). The New York Central Railroad runs 12 trains daily on this route, including the famous Twentieth Century Limited.

141R LIBERATION 2-8-2

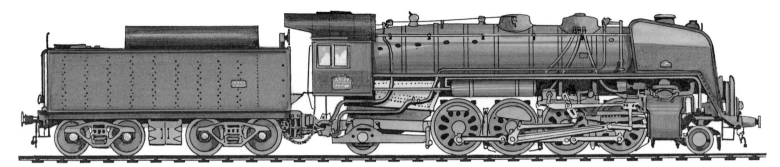

Country of Origin: France
Railway: French National Railways (SNCF)
Date: 1945
Length Overall: 26.161m (79ft 3in)
Total Weight: 18,809kg (413,800lb)
Cylinders: 2 596x711mm (23.5x28in)
Driving Wheels: 1.65m (5ft 5in)
Axle Load: 22,050kg (48,510lb)
Fuel: 10,909kg (24,000lb)
Grate Area: 5.2msq (55.5sq ft)
Water: 1,468lit (6,666gal) (8,000 US gal)
Heating Surface: 251msq (2,699sq ft)
Superheater: 65msq (704sq ft)
Steam Pressure: 1.4kg/cmsq (20psi)
Adhesive Weight: 80,182kg (176,400lb)
Tractive Effort: 20,191kg (44,500lb)

No fewer than 1,340 Class 141R locomotives were built and supplied to SNCF between 1945 and 1947. The construction was spread between Baldwin, Alco, Lima, the Montreal Locomotive Works and the Canadian Locomotive Works. They proved a great success, virtually replacing the entire French railway stock that had been destroyed during the Second World War, and these economical steam locomotives were the last in service with SNCF. Many of the later locomotives became oil-burners.

An SNCF 141R Liberation locomotive at Le Mans in 1968.

WEST COUNTRY CLASS 4-6-2

Country of Origin: Great Britain
Railway: Southern Railway (SR)
Date: 1946
Length Overall: 20.542m (67ft 4.75in)
Total Weight: 138,182kg (304,000lb)
Cylinders: 3 416x610mm (16.7x24in)
Driving Wheels: 1.879m (6ft 2in)
Axle Load: 20,227kg (44,500lb)
Fuel: 5,000kg (11,000lb)
Grate Area: 3.55msq (38.25sq ft)
Water: 24,970lit (5,500gal) (6,600 US gal)
Heating Surface: 197msq (2,122sq ft)
Superheater: 50.6msq (545sq ft)
Steam Pressure: 19.7kg/cmsq (280psi)
Adhesive Weight: 59,545kg (131,000lb)
Tractive Effort: 14,083kg (31,046lb)

A total of 109 West Country Class 4-6-2 locomotives were built as the successors to 31 locomotives of the Merchant Navy Class, and were all built at Southern Railways' Brighton Works except for six. Not a great success, the Class proved expensive to build and to run, although they did haul the prestigious Golden Arrow train from London Victoria to Dover Docks. They remained in service until 1967.

City of Wells *storms through Bentham in a winter scene.*

242 A1 CLASS 4-8-4

Country of Origin: France
Railway: French National Railways (SNCF)
Date: 1946
Length Overall: 17.765m (58ft 3.5in)
Total Weight: 225,455kg (496,000lb)
Cylinders: HP: 1 600x720mm (23.6x28.3in); LP: 2 680x760mm (27x29.9in)
Driving Wheels: 1.95m (6ft 4.75in)
Axle Load: 21,136kg (46,500lb)
Fuel: 11,364kg (25,000lb)
Grate Area: 5msq (54sq ft)
Water: 34,050lit (7,500gal) (9,000 US gal)
Heating Surface: 253msq (2,720sq ft)
Superheater: 120msq (1,249sq ft)
Steam Pressure: 20.4kg/cmsq (290psi)
Adhesive Weight: 84,318kg (185,500lb)

Regarded as André Chapelon's masterpiece, this was the first locomotive to be built in France after the Second World War. It was also France's first 4-8-4 and was based on rebuilding pre-war 4-8-2s but featuring many Chapelon innovations. Unfortunately it was introduced just as the French government had decided to electrify. As a consequence this, the most powerful steam locomotive outside North America, became a one-off despite being extremely fuel-efficient and a match for any diesel or electric locomotive. The locomotive featured a high-pressure cylinder inside, driving the leading main axle plus two low-pressure cylinders outside and driving the second axle; it also included double piston-valves, two thermic syphons in the firebox, a mechanical stoker and a triple Kylchap chimney. Although the locomotive was broken up when withdrawn from service, it has since been rebuilt.

No. 242 A1 was Chapelon's masterpiece and was rebuilt from a pre-war 4-8-2.

Country of Origin: Great Britain
Railway: British Railways (BR)
Date: 1948
Length Overall: 22.25m (73ft)
Total Weight: 167,727kg (369,000lb)
Cylinders: 3 482x660mm (19x26in)
Driving Wheels: 2.032m (6ft 8in)
Axle Load: 22,500kg (49,500lb)
Fuel: 9,091kg (20,000lb)
Grate Area: 4.6msq (50sq ft)
Water: 22,700lit (5,000gal) (6,000 US gal)
Heating Surface: 228.6msq (2,461sq ft)
Superheater: 63.2msq (680sq ft)
Steam Pressure: 17.6kg/cmsq (250psi)
Adhesive Weight: 67,273kg (148,000lb)
Tractive Effort: 16,900kg (37,400lb)

Beautiful, fast, efficient and economical, the 44 Class A1 4-6-2 locomotives of British Railways were a great success. Over a period of 12 years they recorded an average daily distance of 325km (202 miles), and because they required very little maintenance they were able to remain in service right through until the last days of British mainline steam. The A1s were developed from the Class A2 locomotives of which 15 were built immediately after the Second World War under the guidance of Edward Thompson (Sir Nigel Gresley's successor). Thompson was joined by Arthur Peppercorn, and the improvements, refinements and modifications detailed by the Doncaster drawing office led to these highly successful A1s.

No. 60149, Amadis, prepares to depart from King's Cross, London.

C62 CLASS 4-6-4

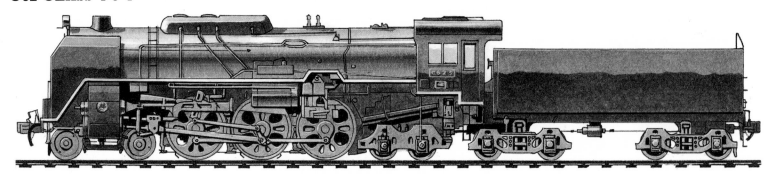

Country of Origin: Japan
Railway: Japanese National Railways (JNR)
Date: 1949
Length Overall: 21.46m (70ft 5in)
Total Weight: 161,818kg (356,000lb)
Cylinders: 2 521x660mm (20.5x26in)
Driving Wheels: 1.75m (5ft 9in)
Axle Load: 16,591kg (36,500lb)
Fuel: 10,000kg (22,000lb)
Grate Area: 3.85msq (41.5sq ft)
Water: 22,019lit (4,850gal) (8,820 US gal)
Heating Surface: 245msq (2,640sq ft)
including super heater
Steam Pressure: 16kg/cmsq (228psi)
Adhesive Weight: 64,773kg (142,500lb)
Tractive Effort: 13,925kg (30,690lb)

Known as 'Swallows', the C62 Class 4-6-4 locomotives were basically rebuilt D52 Mikados which were originally built during the Second World War and were themselves based on a scaled-down version of early Baldwin locomotives. They were used on mainline express trains. Two locomotives have been preserved.

Two C62 Class locomotives head an express train on Hokkaido Island.